Building a Life

Pastor Justin Adams, Author

Dr. Artie Brunson, Contributor

Contents

About Pastor Justin Adams

Pastor Justin Adams is married to Tiffany Adams and together they have two beautiful children. He is a devoted family man. He says, "My family is the most important aspect of my life besides the Lord Jesus Christ."

He loves spending time with his wife and children. Their home is filled with love, laughter, prayer, and forgiveness. He is active in his children's lives and devotes much of his time to their needs and activities.

Pastor Justin began leading NEW LIFE Praise Center over seven years ago, at which time the Lord called him to begin this ministry. Located in downtown Covington, GA, this church has exploded with hundreds of people hearing about the love of God, Grace of Jesus Christ, and the redemptive power of the cross. NEW LIFE's dynamic and enthusiastic worship is matched by the passion and love Pastor Justin has for ministering.

He has many accolades to his credit. He holds a Bachelor of Education degree from Mercer University and also a Master of Theology from Liberty University. He is a true man of God and a spokesman for grace. He is a much sought-after revivalist, teacher, and preacher.

He is an avid spokesperson for those deemed unworthy of church and those who have been shunned by society. He is a man who loves people and believes all should be able to hear the Gospel of our Lord Jesus Christ.

Pastor Justin is also heavily involved in the community. He leads two mentor groups at local schools, serves on the school councils at two local schools, and spends countless hours in discipleship with other men from his church.

Amongst his many accolades, he will tell you his greatest is being the husband of First Lady Tiffany, the father to Charleigh and Levi, and the Pastor of the most loving church, NEW LIFE Praise Center.

About Dr. Artie Brunson

Dr. Artie Brunson enjoys life in Covington, GA where he attends NEW LIFE Praise Center. He serves his church and community in many ways, always finding blessings through helping and serving others.

His studies include the doctoral degree from Liberty University in addition to BS, MEd, and EdS degrees from Georgia College and State University.

He loves to sing, and in quiet moments at home he enjoys reading while relaxing with his pet. Scripture study is an important part of Dr. Brunson's daily routine. His prayer each day is to understand how God's Word applies to his life and to find ways to bless others through what is studied.

Dedication

To my wife: You my dear are so much more than a wife. You are the sounding board to my decisions. The love of my life. The friend I always count on. The caring person in a selfish world. You are my everything. This life is so much better because I get to build this life with you. Our home and our children are blessed because of you.

You support me in prayer and in encouragement. You motivate me to be better. You are my companion and my partner. You are the light in my life and I love you. Years ago, I was a different man and you loved me then. Now, God has molded me and you love me even more. You have stayed by my side through so much. Never behind me or in front, but you have always stayed beside me. You are strong, intelligent, and caring. God broke the mold when He made you. How did I get so lucky?

You are part of God's grace towards me. Grace is when God gives us something we don't deserve. That's you! I don't deserve you but God's grace gave me you. Thank you! Thank you for loving me. Thank you for all the times you share me with our church. Thank you for being such an amazing mom to our children. You care so deeply about our daughter and son, I often just sit back and watch how you love them. Thank you for being my friend. Thank you for all your advice. Thank you for your prayers. Thank you for being a role model. Thank you for everything!

To my children: You see your dad at his best and worst. You see your dad at peace and stress. Yet, somehow, with a simple hug you keep me grounded. I'm so proud of you two. You handle life so well.

To Charleigh: You're beautiful. You're smart. You're funny. Never lose your spunk. I love your wit. I love your charm. I love you. I can't wait to see how God uses you for His Kingdom.

To Levi: My precious son. Your heart is so gentle. You are as innocent as anyone I've ever met. Never lose that. Stay humble and kind my son. They will serve you well in life. I'm proud of you. Grow up to be a "good man." That's all I ask of you. Get ready, God has big plans for you.

To my parents: You never gave up on me. You constantly kept me in your prayers and for this I'm forever thankful. You both loved me when I was unlovable; this is the epitome of faithful parents. Thank you for every single act of parenting, kindness, and care! To this day, your support is so very much appreciated. You give and sacrifice to see my family prosper and the ministry grow. Your selflessness knows no bounds. In my eye, you two are truly Christ-Like! Thank you for being examples to everyone. My children adore you. They are so blessed with you because you both are amazing grandparents.

To NEW LIFE Praise Center: Your support and acknowledgment of our vision is so appreciated. You truly believe in welcoming everyone and allowing everyone a chance to build a life. Thank you for supporting my endeavors and thank you for your service to the ministry and all your work for the kingdom of God.

I enjoy your friendships and your families so very much. Your smiles, your hugs, and your compassion for others move me beyond words. I am overwhelmed by your love for me and my family. I am thankful for your prayers and all of your kind words. I have had the pleasure of attending many churches but there is something special about ours. I think the diversity and the wide array of backgrounds make us who we are. Keep up the good fight and keep growing your faith in Jesus Christ. He is the Hope of the world.

Foreword

This book is presented to all readers, wherever you may be in building a life through your Christian walk.

Maybe you've lived your faith for many years. Let this book remind you about the simplicity of a strong foundation and the power of what you allow in your surroundings.

Maybe you're new in your faith. Read and discover scripture that informs us how the Holy Spirit is a Master Builder of our lives and how God protects us, just as the secure roof of a house provides protection.

Maybe you have questions about the Christian faith and you're interested to learn about it. Reflect on these words as you receive this message about God's grace, mercy, and blessings.

Through Jeremiah 29:11, we hold onto a very special promise: "For I know the plans I have for you, declares the LORD, plans for welfare and not for evil, to give you a future and a hope." Just as an architect has plans before construction begins on a strong building, so too does God have plans for our lives, even before we were born (Jeremiah 1:5).

I pray that you will be blessed from the reading of this book and that the message within these pages will guide you as you're building a life.

Dr. Brunson

The Foundational Principle

Matthew 7:24-27 ESV

Everyone then who hears these words of mine and does them will be like a wise man who built his house on the rock. And the rain fell, and the floods came, and the winds blew and beat on that house, but it did not fall, because it had been founded on the rock. And everyone who hears these words of mine and does not do them will be like a foolish man who built his house on the sand. And the rain fell, and the floods came, and the winds blew and beat against that house, and it fell, and great was the fall of it.

Think about where you live. Whether it's an apartment, a house, an RV, wherever you live, just think about it for a moment.

If I asked you to describe your home to me, you would most likely tell me about the location, the color, the design, the square footage, the size of the lot, and the number of bedrooms.

Do you think about the age of the home? Do you think about the colors of the walls? Do you think about the furnishings inside? You might think about the brick or the stucco. You might think about the hardwood or the tile. You might think about the cabinets and all the different décor. All of these are features of your home, but you probably wouldn't think about the foundation of your home.

Perhaps you don't even know where the foundation of your home is located. Perhaps you've never even inspected the foundation of your home, because the foundation of your home is covered by everything else that you have built. But the first thing that was ever built of your home was its foundation, which you don't see.

The Bible says, *"By wisdom a house is built, and through understanding it is established..." (Proverbs 24:3 NIV).*

A good foundation must be established first. When you understand that you have a good foundation, then you can establish the walls. Then you can establish the roof. This is true not only in your home, but also this is true in your life.

In our opening text, Jesus tells us the parable which contrasts two builders. One was a wise builder who built his house on a good rock, and one was a foolish builder who built his house on sand. Jesus emphasizes how critical it is to have a strong foundation. The use of a building metaphor should not surprise you, because Jesus was a builder—He was a carpenter. Jesus knew the difference between a solid house and a careless one. However, this story is not just for architects, contractors, and carpenters; this story is for you and me.

Building a house is simply an analogy for building a life. And this is the point that Jesus was making. **You are Building a Life**, and the foundation that you choose is the most important feature for your life.

The most important feature of your home is the foundation that you don't even look at. And the most important aspect of your life is a solid foundation.

You can build a life on everything else, but it will fall and you will fail when the storms of life come.

If you build your foundation on The Rock, who is Jesus Christ, when the floods of life come, your house will still be standing.

If you build it on sand, it will fall and you will fail. When the winds of life come, you won't know what to do and you will crumble. The quality of construction of any home, no matter how fancy or elaborate must be built on a solid foundation.

We all want a good life. We all want a comfortable living. Some people want to be rich, and some people just want to have enough money to pay the bills.

I don't see anything wrong with either one; if you want to be rich, then go after it. Some people want to eat lobster, and some people just want enough to eat. Some want to enjoy the finer things of life, while others just simply enjoy having enough. Indeed, nothing is wrong with either one.

However, regardless of the life that you are constructing, if it is not built on a solid foundation, when the storms, the wind, and rains come just like the parable says, your life will fail and your house will have a great fall.

Building on a solid foundation is the key to great construction, and building on a solid foundation is the key to your spiritual life.

We must never forget the foundation that Jesus Christ is Lord of all and His grace is greater than any sin that you've ever committed and everything the world has to offer.

A lot of people build their Christian life on different things. Some people build their Christian life on tithing. And I think it's good to tithe to the church. I think you should give to the church and give freely. The Bible says to give with a joyful heart. Give freely of what you've received. But if you build your relationship with Jesus Christ on finances, then when you don't have any money, you're going to fail.

Some people believe they can build their Christian life on miracles. They come to church for the miracles that they'll receive. I love the miracles. I love when the Spirit of God just miraculously moves in our lives, but if that's all you've got, then you will fail and your house will fall when trials come. The miracle is only for that moment. Life will never be built on miracles alone.

Some people like to build their relationships on the gifts of the Spirit, including healings, miracles, and others found in 1 Corinthians 12. I love all of those things. I love the gifts of the Spirit. I think we need to exercise them in the church, but if that's all you've got for your foundation, then when the gifts are not being exercised and the storms come you fail and your house will fall.

If you'll build upon the rock which is Jesus Christ, if you build on the blood-bought sacrifice of Jesus Christ, if you build upon the cross, if you build upon the nail-scarred hands, then when the storms come it will not fall and you will not fail.

I'm convinced too many believers have got it confused. They're building on goosebumps. They're building on the shouts. They're building on the tears. They're building on miracles. Don't get me wrong—I love all those things. I love to shout! I love to cry! I love the miracles! But we need to love the Giver of these things, Jesus Christ, more!

If you never shout another day in your life you still have Jesus. If you never exercise the gifts of the Spirit another day in your life, you still have Jesus. If you never experience a healing, you still have Jesus. You will always have Jesus! It's that foundation that makes the difference.

Jesus Christ—Him as the foundation—changed my life. It wasn't the miracles or the goosebumps or the shouts or the crying, even though I believe in those things, because I can find them in the Word of God. It was Jesus who changed my life.

Think about it: a scary movie can give you goosebumps. You can shout at a ball game. But these will never last. Our Christian lives must be built on Jesus as the foundation.

My church recently had a Wednesday night service and we prayed for the healing of several people. The next day two of them called me with praises of their healings; these are real examples of real miracles and answered prayers.

I love miracles and I believe in them, but that healing won't get you into Heaven. It's Jesus Christ who will. That's the foundation. The healings and the miracles are the walls we build around the foundation.

One of the prerequisites that I have when people come to me for marriage counseling—whether the marriage is in trouble or whether the couple is ready to develop a deeper understanding of one another—is the couple must both attend church for at least four weeks in a row, every Sunday. They must do this for four weeks in a row because I believe this: after their church attendance and after hearing the sacrifice of Jesus Christ every Sunday for a month, they can understand when the Bible says, *"Husbands, love your wives, just as Christ loved the church and gave himself up for her" (Ephesians 5:25 NIV).*

Think about it. The meaning of the foundation you have in your marriage is love. If you build your foundation on anything else, it will not last. If relationships are built on anything other than the foundation of Jesus Christ as Lord, then husbands will not be able to love their wives the way they are intended. We must understand the love Christ has for His church.

There is no way for you to love your wife properly, and there is no way for you to love your husband properly, until you find out what love really is, and that love is a sacrificial love that reflects Christ in your life.

Think about this: Do you have great kids? Would you love to have great kids? Would you love to have well-mannered kids who will be upstanding citizens? Don't you want to have good children as they grow up?

The Bible is filled with power-packed principles—foundational principles—of how we are to parent our children.

If you're trying to parent without the Word of God, then you're building upon a shaky foundation.

Think about this: Would you like to have money to blow? Would you like to have extra money? We all want to have a nice life. We all want to be financially stable. Some of us even want to be rich. Some of us want millions of dollars; that's fine. Some of us just want to have enough money to change the oil when it's due. You can try and try to build your house on finances, but if the foundation of your home is on finances then it will fall and you will fail when the storms come. If our foundation is on anything other than the solid rock of Jesus Christ, you will not be able to stand. When you have a foundation that is firm, that is found on Jesus Christ, the wind can howl. The rain can come.

The thunder can roll. The lightning can strike. However, your life will not be moved. The enemy can throw his best at you, but you have a foundation. The Bible says we should be like a tree planted by the water. You might sway slightly in the hard winds, but you will not be moved.

We must build on the foundation who is Jesus Christ. That foundation is sure. That foundation is certain. That foundation is solid. It's steady. It's stable. It's unchanging. He's the same yesterday, today and forever. He's the foundation that doesn't change in your life; He's the foundation that changes your life.

There is a story which reminds us of the importance of a solid foundation. There was a wealthy man who was leaving for an extended vacation. He had a contractor that had worked for him for years. He said to the contractor, "While I am away, I want you to build me a fine new home according to these plans. Build me the nicest home you've ever built. Be sure to work with extreme care and use the best of everything. Spare no expense in building this new home."

During the process, the contractor discovered an easy opportunity to substitute inferior materials in the foundation. And he put in his pocket the money that he saved. He thought, "You know, the rich man will never inspect the foundation. I'll go ahead and decorate with the best of materials. I'll put in granite countertops and stainless steel appliances. I'll spend what was expected on the inside, because it can be seen. However, I'll keep the money I would have spent on a quality foundation, because he won't see it anyway. He will never know the difference."

The contractor knew the man would never inspect the foundation. After all, it's hidden by the décor.

He thought his plan was a foolproof way to prosper and profit.

Upon his return, the wealthy man inspected the new home. He looked around and said, "You built it exactly the way I wanted. It looks great. It's the perfect color. It's the perfect size, with all the perfect furniture and equipment. Everything looks great, and you spared no expense. You've worked for me for over 20 years, and in appreciation for all your years of service, now I'm giving you this house. Because you've worked so diligently for me all these years, this home is now yours. Here's the deed."

All the contractor could do was lower his head in shame, for he remembered the inferior foundation.

Think about this: we are building for eternity, not for looks. You and I are **Building a Life**, not only for this life but the one to come. The contractor had every nice thing in the home, but it was built on a poor foundation. We all know the only way to fix a poor foundation is to tear it all down and start over. The contractor knew what was going to happen when the strong winds were to come.

This is abundantly true for some of us. We are not built on solid foundations in our lives. When everything is sunny, our houses can stand. But when all Hell comes against us, it will fall and we will fail because we have not built on the solid foundation of Jesus Christ. **Without Him, nothing else matters.**

We can decorate our lives. We can build and build, but if our foundations are not secure, we are going to fail and our house will fall. Are you building with inferior materials, or are you building with the choice material, Jesus Christ?

Don't ever forget that receiving our Heavenly mansion later depends on the foundation of our earthly life now. Nothing else matters. It's the foundational principle.

Jesus, I speak Your name in praise and in thankfulness for all of Your promises. I thank You for Your abundant love which never ends. I thank You for my salvation which I could never deserve. You have changed my life. Please let others see the good work You have started in me. Thank you, Jesus. Amen.

Reflections

The Master Builder

1 Corinthians 3:10-11 NASB

"According to the grace of God which was given to me, like a wise master builder I laid a foundation, and another is building on it. But each man must be careful how he builds on it. For no man can lay a foundation other than the one which is laid, which is Jesus Christ."

Are you a contractor? Do you know a contractor or a builder? Have you ever helped with building a house? Have you ever seen the process of a house being built? What is the first thing you have to do when you build a home? The first thing you build is the foundation. You must lay the foundation before you can build the walls. You must lay the foundation before you can put the ceiling and the roof on the house. Most of the time, the foundation is hidden. Most of the time, people do not even look at the foundation.

But the Bible say that when the rains come, and the winds blow, and the floods come, and they beat against the house, if it does not have a solid foundation it will fall. I want to compare that to your spiritual life. If you don't have a solid foundation which is Jesus Christ, when the rains come, the floods come, the winds come, and it beats against your house, it will fall and you will fail. However if you are built on the Rock, which is Jesus Christ, the winds can blow, the rains can fall, but you will stand!

In the first chapter of this study, we learned about building the foundation. In this chapter, let's learn about building upward. You can't hang a picture if you don't have a wall. You can't put a couch in the room unless you've first made the floor. Let's talk about the Master Builder. As I began to study the

Word of God in preparation for this message, I considered this question: If Jesus is the foundation, then who's building our lives? The Master Builder, which is the Holy Spirit.

The Holy Spirit is building something in you. The foundation is Jesus Christ. But the Master Builder—that which leads me and guides me and points me in the right direction—is the Holy Spirit. The Holy Spirit always has as His first assignment and first priority, to point you back to the foundation.

Think about it. When you build a foundation then you build the walls, they are anchored in the foundation. Everything that is surrounding the building points to the foundation, and the Spirit of God is pointing back to the Foundation.

Let's consider this together and learn together. The Spirit of God is not miracles, even though that is a result of the Spirit of God. The Spirit of God is not faith, even though the Bible says that is a gift of the Spirit. The Spirit of God is not wisdom or knowledge, even though the Bible says those are a result of the Spirit. The Spirit of God is not speaking in tongues, even though that is a result of the Spirit. The Spirit of God is not healings, it is not tears, it is not a shout. But the Spirit of God is what points us back to the Foundation.

Let's consider what Jesus said. He said when the Spirit comes, He will teach you all things and bring all things to your remembrance—that means He's pointing you back to the direction of the foundation. And remember Jesus told us He is the Way, the Truth, and the Life. The Spirit proceeded from the Father. What does the Spirit do? The Spirit testifies of Jesus Christ. The Spirit always points you back to the Foundation.

John 14:26 KJV

"But the Comforter, which is the Holy Ghost, whom the Father will send in my name, He shall teach you all things, and bring all things to your remembrance, whatsoever I have said unto you."

John 15:26 GNV

"But when that Comforter shall come, whom I will send unto you from the Father, even the Spirit of truth, which proceedeth of the Father, He shall testify of me."

If all your spirit does is make you speak in tongues, if all your spirit does is give you faith, if all your spirit does is make you shout a little bit, if your spirit only does these things, you don't have the Holy Spirit; you have a personal spirit.

But if you have the Spirit of God, it will always point you back to Jesus Christ!

I like to shout! I like to get excited! I like when someone is used in the gifts of the Spirit. I like it when someone speaks prophecy. However, if that's all you have, then you have your own fleshly spirit. You need the Spirit of God to point you back to the Foundation. It is the Spirit of God that points us back and then brings these gifts.

The Spirit points us in the right direction.

All of the other things which come with having the Spirit are byproducts of the Spirit. The Bible says I wish you all would speak in tongues. I wish you all would prophesy. It doesn't tell you not to do those things. But the Spirit's first assignment is to point you back to the Foundation. The Spirit testifies of Jesus Christ. Jesus said when we receive the Spirit of God, we receive two things.

Acts 1:8 NIV

"But you will receive power when the Holy Spirit comes on you; and you will be my witnesses in Jerusalem, and in all Judea and Samaria, and to the ends of the earth."

You will receive power and you shall be witnesses of Jesus to everyone. The only reason I have the power and the only reason I can shout, and the only reason I can dance, and the only reason I am saved is because of Jesus Christ!

The Holy Spirit's first priority and assignment is to point us to Jesus Christ. Think about it like this: God the Father sent God the Son. God the Son ascended—went up into Heaven—and then God the Son sent God the Spirit to descend and be among us. And this why the Spirit of God points to Jesus.

Matthew 28:18 King James 2000 Bible

"And Jesus came and spoke unto them, saying, 'All power is given unto Me in Heaven and in earth.'"

Jesus is so important that all power is given to Him. The Holy Spirit is with us constantly to direct us back to Jesus in all things. The Spirit of God—the Spirit of Christ—always points us to Jesus, where all power is found.

The Spirit of God always points you back to the sacrificial foundation of Jesus Christ, because the Spirit of God knows when the rains come, the floods come, the winds blow, and they beat upon your house, your house will not fall and you will not fail if you have the Foundation of Jesus Christ.

Matthew 7:25 NASB

"And the rain fell, and the floods came, and the winds blew and slammed against that house; and

yet it did not fall, for it had been founded on the rock."

The Bible says the rains came. The floods came. The winds blew. And they all beat against the house. The house was rocking from the storm. It seems like everywhere you turn, you have something in front of you, something behind you, and something on each side of you. And they're beating on you. You cry, "Lord, I can't get out of the storm! Everywhere I go, there is something on me!" But the Spirit of God will keep you from falling because you are on the Foundation of Jesus! Let it blow! Let the rains fall! Jesus is my foundation! I will not be moved!

If you're built on the foundation, on Jesus Christ, they can rock your boat. They can knock you around. But your feet will not move. Because you are on the Foundation.

The Spirit of God empowers us to build.

In the Bible, the Spirit of God is described as breath and also as wind. The Bible teaches you cannot see the Spirit of God. I want you to notice when the Spirit of God was first recognized as in the 'building business.'

Genesis 1:1-2 NIV
"In the beginning God created the heavens and the earth. Now the earth was formless and empty, darkness was over the surface of the deep, and the Spirit of God was hovering over the waters."

The Spirit of God was there. Just waiting to build something. Just waiting for God to give the word and then building life would begin. How did God do it? He spoke it into existence. He said let there be life. Every time God speaks, it's the Spirit of God. His breath is the Spirit of God. The Spirit not only points us to the Foundation, but without it in your life you will not be able to build upward. Your building will be incomplete.

Genesis 2:7 KJV
"And the LORD God formed man of the dust of the ground, and breathed into his nostrils the breath of life; and man became a living soul."

Before man could rise—before he could sit up and be alive—before he could exist, God had to breathe into his life. Without the Spirit of God in your life, you will not rise up. You will never flourish in your faith. But when you receive the Spirit of God, you receive life!

We became living when the Spirit of God began to build.

Ephesians 2:22 NIV
"And in him you too are being built together to become a dwelling in which God lives by His Spirit."

The same God then is the same God now. He wants to lay the foundation in your life and He wants to breathe life into your spiritual walk. He reminds you that He is coming to live with you!

Think about it: God laid the foundation which is Jesus Christ. The Holy Spirit is building you. But why? So God can live with you. God can live on the inside.

The omnipresent, omnipotent God, Creator of light and darkness, Creator of Heaven and earth, wants to live inside of me! He wants a relationship with me!

It's not about the rules of religion; it's about His relationship with me!

The Old Testament prophets did not have God living on the inside of them. Moses didn't have God dwelling on the inside of him. King David didn't have God dwelling on the inside of him. King Saul, Prophet Samuel, Abraham, Isaac, Jacob, none of them ever had God dwelling on the inside of them, because the Bible says the Spirit hadn't descended yet.

So, what happened?

Acts 2:2-4 NKJV
"And suddenly there came a sound from heaven, as of a rushing mighty wind, and it filled the whole house where they were sitting. Then there appeared to them divided tongues, as of fire, and one sat upon each of them. And they were all filled with the Holy Spirit and began to speak with other tongues, as the Spirit gave them utterance."

On the day of Pentecost, they were all together in prayer. They were in one place and in one accord. They all had their minds alike. They all had the same thing in common. They weren't worried about the stress of life. They weren't worried about the distractions of fear. They were only and completely focused on Jesus Christ. Then the Spirit of God came like a rushing, mighty wind.

The Spirit of God came.

Jude 1:20 KJV
"But ye, beloved, building up yourselves on your most holy faith, praying in the Holy Ghost..."

The Spirit of God builds us and our prayer is crucial. They were all there praying. Too many of us want to try and build that house on our own. But we are not praying in the Spirit. Because when I'm tired, the Spirit strengthens me. When I'm weak, the Spirit encourages me. When I can't find the inspiration to pray, the Bible says the Spirit will make intercession for me. When I'm broken, the Spirit mends me. When I am downtrodden, the Spirit picks me up. When my life is falling apart, I've got a Master Builder. The Holy Spirit will build me up!

When I don't know what to pray, I'll pray to the Spirit. Because the Spirit is building something in me. The Spirit of God will not quit. The Spirit of God will not let you quit, because the Spirit of God is the Builder. The Bible infers the Spirit is the Master Builder, and the builder doesn't not stop until the project is finished.

You are not finished yet. You and I are not done yet. You still have people to reach. You've got things to say and people to love on. We have souls to lead to Christ and people to reach. You've got people to talk to. You've got people to love on. We're not going to stop until everyone knows the love of God!

Philippians 1:6 NIV

"...being confident of this, that he who began a good work in you will carry it on to completion until the day of Christ Jesus."

I'm confident in this: that God began to build something in me and in you, and He will complete it. You can decorate it all you want to. You can make it look as fancy as you want; God's not working on our outside. He began the good work in me and you. He'll keep building until it's complete or until Christ Jesus comes back. Let Him build.

God didn't tell you to get it right first and then come to Him. He said He will clean you up from the inside.

The Spirit of God empowers us to build, and it is built on our Foundation which is Jesus Christ, but it's the Holy Spirit which builds.

I thank God for building me, for building in me.

Thank God for building in you, too.

Heavenly Father, I thank You for the work You have started in my life. You love me even when I feel unlovable. You forgave me even before I did wrong. You accept me, even though You know all my flaws and faults. Your mercy has kept me safe from things I'll never even know, and Your beautiful grace continues to bless me as I am growing closer to You. Thank You for Your precious, never-ending love. Amen.

Reflections

The Decorations

We've learned a house must have a solid foundation. Your life must have one too, a foundation built on Jesus Christ. Once you have it, let the troubles come. You'll still be standing.

We've learned how the Spirit of God is a builder. It builds in your life.

1 Corinthians 3:10 NASB
"According to the grace of God which was given to me, like a wise master builder I laid a foundation, and another is building on it..."

The Spirit of God builds on your foundation. The Spirit of God always builds up, and it always points back down to your foundation. Everything that the Spirit of God does points to the foundation, which is Jesus Christ.

Now let's think about how your home—and how your life—is decorated. What does your home look like? Take a moment to really think of lots of details about your home's decorations.

Think of a room inside your home, maybe your living room or your family room. Is there a couch? Are there chairs? Are pictures hanging on the walls? Is there a table? Are there flowers in the room? Is there a rug?

1 Kings 8:13 ESV
"I have indeed built you an exalted house, a place for you to dwell in forever."

Why are you building a house right now—why are you building a spiritual home?

You are building a place so God can dwell. That's the whole reason we learned about the foundation, and the whole reason we learned about the Spirit of God who builds upward. And it's the whole reason we are going to learn about decorating your home.

Think about the people who live with you, or think about the people with whom you'd like to share your home. Think about how you would decorate your home together. You might think about a picture of a favorite vacation memory. You might think of a photo of your family. You might think of the fire place and the times your family enjoyed it. You might think of the cherished family Bible placed on the coffee table. These are the things I think about in my home. Everything which my family decorates with reminds us of something.

Everything we put in our home is there to point us to love.

What you put in your home—what you look at day in and day out—means a lot.

What you do day in and day out at your home means a lot.

If you and I look in your home and look at your walls, we will begin to understand what you see every day means a lot; what you have in your life means a lot. And we can compare the decorations in our homes to the way we are decorating and enhancing our spiritual life.

What are you decorating your life with?

We've got a solid foundation—it's Jesus Christ.

We've got the Spirit of God. It's beginning to build upward in our lives—like the walls in our homes are built.

So, what are you decorating with?

Think about moving into a new home or seeing a brand new home or apartment, and when you walk in, it is completely empty. The first thing you start doing is thinking about the decorations. "Wow, the couch would look good right there. Oh, I know exactly where we're going to put the TV. We're going to put our shelves here. Pictures of the family would look good here." If you ever go into an empty home, the first thing we start to do is think about how you are going to decorate.

The reason you start to decorate is because your house is not complete until it's furnished. Think about it. **You don't want to live in an empty house.** You want it decorated. And you want your spiritual life decorated and filled with grace and mercy.

Grace is God blessing you, regardless if you deserve it or not. You want your life decorated with grace.

You also want your spiritual life decorated with mercy. Mercy is God withholding something that you DO deserve. God's mercy is saying I will NOT punish you, even though you DO deserve it.

You can't have God's blessing without God withholding some punishment. Thank God for the cross of Jesus Christ, because that is where grace and mercy are. Even though we deserved our punishment, He kept it from us and took it for us.

God said, "Even though you deserve it, I'll take your punishment and put it on my Son." Praise God for His grace and mercy!

We all like grace and mercy in our lives. Grace looks good in my house! Mercy looks good in my house! I want my spiritual life full of God's blessings! I praise God that He didn't punish me. I praise God that He didn't send me to Hell but He saved my soul. I praise God that I'm still walking. It's only by the grace and mercy of God that I'm not dead. A common problem is this: even though we love God's grace and mercy, we don't want to share it.

I love when people come over to my house. I love when friends come over to hang out. I love to entertain. However if we have grace and mercy in our homes, yet when people come over we don't show them hospitality, they'll stop coming over. It's the same thing in the church.

If you weren't shown grace and mercy when you first came to church, then you wouldn't have returned. If I didn't show you grace and mercy—if I didn't show you what God has done for me—you wouldn't keep coming.

Your friends and family are not going to accompany you to church if you don't extend the same grace and mercy that God has extended to you.

I remember my past. I remember all the bad, sinful things I've done. I remember who I used to be. I also remember when God's grace and mercy came into my life. I remember how God's grace and mercy changed me—changed a sinner—and that same grace and mercy can take a man out of a ditch and put him on the Rock, which is Jesus Christ. Praise God for His grace and mercy!

Even Jesus had His house decorated with grace.

John 1:14 NIV
"The Word became flesh and made his dwelling among us. We have seen his glory, the glory of the one and only Son, who came from the Father, full of grace and truth."

The word of God teaches us grace and mercy are eternal.

Psalm 23:6 ESV
"Surely goodness and mercy shall follow me all the days of my life and I will dwell in the house of the Lord Forever."

How long is goodness (grace) and mercy going to follow me? All the days of my life. Forever. Grace and mercy are there when You fall down. You get back up with God's grace and mercy. They stay with us through our final moment of life, and when life ends and we are buried in the grave, the Bible says to be absent of the body is to be present with the Lord, then grace and mercy follow me for eternity.

We've got to decorate our homes with grace and mercy! You have to put these things in your house. Put one up on one wall, and one up on the other. We've got to decorate our church with grace and mercy! We have to decorate our lives with grace and mercy!

In Heaven, there's a throne. It's so important that the throne of Jesus Christ is called grace. And grace is what Jesus sits on. Grace is in Heaven.

Once you start to pray, the first things you get are grace and mercy, and you get them in your time of need. We need them every day. I need His grace when I fall down. I need His grace when I wake up. I need His grace when I lay down. I need His grace when I pray. I need it in my work. I need it in my children. I need it in my marriage. I need it in my bank account. I need God's grace and mercy every day, so praise God that I can touch the throne room of Heaven with grace on one side and mercy on the other.

Hebrews 4:16 NIV
"Let us then approach God's throne of grace with confidence, so that we may receive mercy and find grace to help us in our time of need."

As you are decorating your home—your spiritual life—with grace and mercy, you also need to decorate it with forgiveness.

There are people who talk bad about others. There are people who steal from others. People cheat others. People lie to others. People betray others. Perhaps these things have happened to you. It makes you mad, angry, and disappointed.

How long do you stay that way? How long do you hold onto those feelings of anger? What happens to you while you keep those feelings?

A better question is to ask what happens when you forgive.

See, forgiveness isn't really for the other person. Your forgiveness towards him is not for him; it's for you. It truly releases you from the anger. When you forgive him, you allow him to be removed from your thinking, removed from your conscience, removed from your anxiety and your fear. Our

hatred toward him is all gone, and now we have

something beautiful in its place to look at.

However if you hold on to it, it will dominate your

thinking, and you will allow the ugliness of

unforgiveness to move into your home. But when

you invite forgiveness into your home, you decide

to release them and to free yourself.

Think about your children. Around noon, they start

acting up. By the afternoon, you've had enough

and it's time for discipline! Then by bedtime

they're becoming tired and they crawl beside you to

sleep, hugging on you. Do you know why that hug

is so tight? Because children don't hold grudges.

Their love is unconditional. They don't stay mad.

One day they have conflict with their friends; the

next day they are friends again. They have so much

forgiveness in their hearts that they don't hold on

to resentment. Like Jesus said, "You must come to

me as like little children." There's so much forgiveness in a child's heart.

You don't have time to let grudges live in your home.

In a child's heart there's no hatred, no bigotry, no envy, no grudges, because those things don't belong there. Neither do they belong in the hearts of their parents. We need to be better than that. We need to give forgiveness in our lives.

Luke 6:36-37 NKJV
"Therefore be merciful, just as your Father also is merciful. Judge not, and you shall not be judged. Condemn not, and you shall not be condemned. Forgive, and you will be forgiven."

To really understand the significance of these verses in our lives, we need to consider the verse which comes next.

Luke 6:38 NKJV
"Give, and it will be given to you: good measure, pressed down, shaken together, and running over will be put into your bosom. For with the same measure that you use, it will be measured back to you."

Sometimes we read that verse in the context of money. But think about it in the context of forgiveness. When you forgive and when you give mercy to others, God will press down and give even that much more mercy and forgiveness to you. For the same measure that you judge will be the same measure with which you will be judged. We've got to decorate our lives with forgiveness.

We also have to decorate our lives with good thoughts.

What are the things you think about? What do you focus your thoughts on the most?

There are ways to quickly find out. You can look at your bank statements. Typically, the more money you spend on something is what you most often think about. The biggest part of your budget is what you think about the most. Another way is for me to spend about 24 hours with you, and we can find out what you think about. Another way is for us to look at your house and see what your decorations are.

Your house might be decorated with pictures of your children and family.

Pictures control our thoughts. What you look at the most controls your thoughts. What you dwell on the most is what you think about. What things do you watch on the internet? What thing are you viewing online? The things you keep in front of you are the things you keep in your thoughts.

Think about your mind. Think about your heart. And think about sin. Before an act of sin occurs, it first starts in your mind. For example, a person doesn't go from a happy marriage to committing adultery in one moment. What happens is they begin to think about it. It enters their mind first.

You don't backslide or use drugs or drink and drive spontaneously. Before you sin—greed, gluttony, lust, envy, malice, strife, back-biting, gossip, all of those things—it starts with a thought.

Then when you think about it and dwell on it, it goes to your heart. You think about it over and over and over, and it resides in your heart. The Bible says, "Out of the abundance of the heart, the mouth speaks." This is where sin happens. But we have something we can do.

2 Corinthians 10:5 KJV
"...bringing into captivity every thought to the obedience of Christ..."

Tell yourself, "NO I will not think those things. I rebuke them."

You can stop it long before it gets to the point of committing that sin. Bring every thought into captivity.

Notice the Bible didn't say you can stop the thinking.

If I say "RED APPLE" you will probably see the image of a red apple in your mind right now. You cannot stop what you think. But the Bible says you can control it by bringing it into captivity.

I can't stop what I think. Random thoughts come in my mind. Weird things come in my mind, and I can't stop them from popping in there. But I can stop how long I think about it. I can control how long I dwell on things, that way it will not develop into an act of sin. As you dwell on it more and more, your chances of sin increase dramatically. However, if you'll take every thought into captivity and make them obedient to Christ, you can stop sin before it happens in your life.

Some people feel that preaching must always be about Hell being hot. You already know that. I don't want to preach people into Hell; I want to preach them into Heaven! And if you're raising children and all you do is tell them what not to do, you're only half-parenting. And just like God, He's a full parent. I don't tell my children not to do something over and over. Instead, I tell them not to do it and then I tell them what TO do over and over.

I want them to not only reach my expectations but to exceed them. That's the same thing as the Bible. It tells you what not to do, but it also tells you what to decorate with.

Philippians 4:8 CEB
"From now on, brothers and sisters, if anything is excellent and if anything is admirable, focus your thoughts on these things: all that is true, all that is holy, all that is just, all that is pure, all that is lovely, and all that is worthy of praise."

You want to decorate your home with these things, things which are true and holy and pure and lovely. Decorate your home with grace and mercy and forgiveness and good thoughts. Put those things in your home.

In life, we are so used to the decorations that we already have. We decorate our homes with our past, with our sins, with our guilt, and with our shame. We are so used to these things in our homes we can't even imagine having things which are lovely and pure; we are so used to the other things in our lives.

Remember this: the grace and mercy of God is more beautiful and lovely than anything, and they will cover any sin, any guilt, and any shame. God's grace and mercy is bright and vibrant and you can't see the sin through it. It covers it. It covers you. It is the love, it is the blood, it is the sacrifice of Jesus Christ, and everything that was decorated in sin is now covered with things which are beautiful.

The cross is the place where you can come as you are. It is the place where you can lay down your burdens and your shame. Lay down those ugly decorations you've had in your life for far too long.

Allow God to absorb those things, and allow God to decorate with grace and mercy and forgiveness so you can have good thoughts. His grace and mercy and forgiveness will be the most beautiful decorations for you as you are building a life.

Lord, I come to You with a thankful heart, knowing that You have a plan for my life. I pray You'll allow me to always be open to Your Holy Spirit and to be aware of the people and things in my life. Protect me from influences which could take my eyes off You. Help me learn to forgive others who do wrong to me, and remind me of the forgiveness You have already given me. Help me to see the good in others and to remember that Your love is immeasurably greater than any mistake I could ever make. You are so good to me. Amen.

Reflections

The Covering

In the previous chapters, we've compared our spiritual life to building a home. We know we have to have a solid foundation, built upon Jesus Christ. We know the Holy Spirit builds upward within our lives. We know about the decorations of our spiritual life, including grace, mercy, forgiveness, and control over our thoughts.

However, a house is not complete without a roof, and your spiritual life is not complete without a spiritual covering.

Psalm 91:1-2 NIV
"Whoever dwells in the shelter of the Most High will rest in the shadow of the Almighty. I will say of the LORD, 'He is my refuge and my fortress, my God, in whom I trust.'"

If you are looking for words to pray when you go to bed at night or get up in the morning, hold onto Psalm 91 and begin to repeat those words. I'll be under Your shadow, God. God, You are my refuge and my fortress. I trust in You.

When God covers you, the first thing He does is gives you protection. You are protected under God. God is watching over you. You need to understand this before I go on: the story in Psalm 57 reminds us that God protects us from calamity, not from problems.

God protects you from destruction, not from obstacles.

Just because you're going through something doesn't mean that God isn't protecting you. Just because you're in the battle doesn't mean God isn't protecting you. The fact you're still standing in the battle is the sign God is still protecting you. The fact you're still breathing, even though you're going through some mess, lets you know you're protected. The reason you are still fighting, the reason you can still stand up, even when you are going through all kinds of Hell, is because God is protecting you.

No matter what comes your way, God is still protecting you.

Just because you go through the valley doesn't mean God's not protecting you from the obstacles that are around you. Look what happens in Psalm 57. David wrote this at a time when he was fearful for his life. King Saul was chasing David, and David actually wrote this Psalm while he was in the cave hiding from somebody trying to kill him. He wrote this:

Psalm 57:1 ESV

"Be merciful to me, O God, be merciful to me, for in You my soul takes refuge; in the shadow of Your wings I will take refuge, till the storms of destruction pass by."

He didn't ask God to stop the calamity. He said he would be there until he is finished going through them.

I'm going to stay here, God, until these storms pass me by. Yes, I know I have to go through some junk. Yes, I might have to be in a ditch line. Yes, I may fall. Yes, I may suffer. But I'm here under the covering of God. I'll pray under the protection. And I know You will keep me safe. At this time, David had not committed adultery. At this time in David's life, he was the best David he had ever been.

Have you ever felt like that—like you are the best you that you have ever been? You are living right. You're talking right. You're doing good, you quit bad habits. You're getting better. You're sinning less. You're judging less. You're loving more. You're raising your children right and have them in church. You're praying more than you ever have. You're coming to church more than you ever have.

But all of a sudden, all Hell comes against you. And you want to say, "God, what's going on? I've been doing everything right. I've been talking right and walking right. God I'm living the best that I have ever been, and yet I'm still facing these problems."

And God is saying, "I am your protection. I will not deliver you from problems, but I will protect you from destruction."

You see, this is why we let kids fall down on their bicycles. A little bit of problems and a little bit of hurt can teach them something.

God's letting you fall down a little bit, but He's protecting you from destruction. He's protecting from that which will kill you. Even though you go through the valley of the shadow of death, death cannot attack you.

2 Corinthians 4:8-9 NKJV
"We are hard-pressed on every side, yet not crushed; we are perplexed, but not in despair; persecuted, but not forsaken; struck down, but not destroyed..."

Remember, your covering is from above. But on every side, we are hard-pressed. No matter how much presses against you from every side, you must remember and acknowledge that you will not be destroyed because you are protected with the covering of God. Everything that comes at you comes from around you. Think of the word *circumstance*, and the word *circumference,* meaning "around you." Your circumstances are the things happening around you. This is where the devil operates.

The devil operates down here around you, because he is no match up there above you. The devil likes to attack you on your playing field, because the devil thinks that he is as powerful as you are.

But he knows that he is not as powerful as the Most High God. My strength comes from above! The devil cannot touch me from above.

David said, "I'm doing everything right, God, but I need your protection."

You might stumble. You might fall down. You might lose faith. You might lose power. You might grow angry. You might get depressed. You might have anxiety. But the Bible teaches it will not come from above. You will not be struck down. The enemy is on your playing field and no match for God's level. The enemy will never be able to come over the top of you because God's blessing is covering you. You are protected. Thank God right now for protecting you.

You are covered under the protection of God and you're also under the anointing of God. Let's learn where Jesus was under the anointing.

Luke 4:18 NIV
"The Spirit of the Lord is on me, because He has anointed me to proclaim good news to the poor. He

has sent me to proclaim freedom for the prisoners and recovery of sight for the blind, to set the oppressed free..."

Jesus didn't come to judge you. He didn't come to condemn you. He said He came to preach the gospel to the poor, to heal those in need of healing and to set free those who are captive and put down.

You are not put down any more. You have the covering on top of you. You have the anointing of the Holy Spirit in your life. The same Spirit which was on Jesus is the same spirit which is on you. It's the same Holy Spirit; there's not two of them. It's the same Spirit that is now residing in His believers. And He says that it is on you.

I understand that you are not Jesus, but you are His hands and feet. You are not Jesus, but you are His workers. You are not Jesus, but you are His disciples. You are not Jesus, and you cannot do the things He did, but He said "Greater things than these shall you do."

If Jesus Christ is your Lord and Savior, the Bible says that we are His workmanship.
We are created to do good works by His anointing.
We are under the anointing of God.

Joel 2:28 ESV
"And it shall come to pass afterward, that I will pour out My Spirit on all flesh..."

If He was planning to pour it to your side, He would have said so. But He said He will pour it out ON you.

You need to recognize this—the word "pour" is significant.

He doesn't dab a little on you. He doesn't sprinkle it on you. He doesn't give it sparingly on you. The Bible says that He says, "I will POUR out on you." That means when you receive the Spirit of God, you receive all of the Spirit of God, the entire Spirit of God.

Then we learn about and how to use the Spirit in our lives and how to operate in it, but rest assured, the Spirit of God—the anointing of God—is covering you.

It is all on you. There are no ifs, ands, or buts about it. Once you have the Spirit of God, God gives you every bit of it. You can operate under the Spirit of the anointing. You don't have to wait on your time. You're under the anointing of God.

The only way we can accomplish anything for God is to do everything under the anointing.

Zechariah 4:6 NIV

"This is the word of the LORD to Zerubbabel: 'Not by might nor by power, but by my Spirit...'"

It was God's Spirit when He breathed life. The Bible says that Adam did not have a living soul until God breathes the breath of life. The disciples did not have the Spirit of God until all of a sudden there was a sound from Heaven like a rushing, mighty wind. And it filled the house where they were sitting.

You cannot accomplish what God has set out for you to do in the kingdom unless you are covered under the anointing of the Holy Spirit.

Stop right now and remind yourself, "I am anointed."

God, I declare your greatness and I praise you for the Holy Spirit in my life. Protect me and keep me in Your will. I know You will guide my steps and always be with me; touch my heart daily and remind me to come to You with an open heart filled with prayers and praise. I am anointed because I am Your child. Thank You for loving me unconditionally. Amen.

You can be anointed and protected at the same time. Actually, you are protected because first you are anointed.

1 Chronicles 16:22 NASB
"Do not touch My anointed ones, And do My prophets no harm."

Your enemies can talk all they want, but they can't touch you. They can criticize you and persecute you, but they can't touch you. **Because you are anointed.** You are protected. Your enemies can do you no harm. Because you are under the covering and the anointing of God.

People ask me all the time, "Pastor, why is your church so prosperous?" Our church has grown tremendously in a very short amount of time, and we view every person not as a number but as a soul. And we want to love on everyone. We do care about each person.

And I'm asked, "What are you doing that is different than my church?"

I always reply, "We still preach Jesus," and they respond, "We still do, too." I say, "We still sing Amazing Grace," and they respond, "We still do, too." I ask, "But are you under the anointing of God?"

If your church, or your life, or your marriage is prospering, it is under the anointing of God. If you want your marriage to flourish, you can bring your wife all the flowers you want to, but the flowers are going to die. You can cook all you want, but inevitably she is not going to like something you cooked. However when your marriage is under the anointing of God; you talk about God, you fellowship about God, and you enjoy God together. Your marriage can withstand all of Hell's trials when it is under the anointing.

You have to operate under the anointing, and once you do you will be protected because God says, "Don't even touch those who I have anointed."

If you're covered under the anointing of God, and if you're covered by the protection of God, there's one reason why: it's because you're under His blood. There is only one way to receive His protection and His anointing: it is because of the blood of Jesus Christ.

At the Last Supper, He said:

Mark 14:24 NIV

"This is my blood of the covenant, which is poured out for many…"

A covenant is a promise. It is an agreement with you. If God has poured out His blood, that means His blood has covered you if you have asked Him into your life.

Ephesians 1:7 NIV

"In Him (Jesus) we have redemption through His blood, the forgiveness of sins, in accordance with the riches of God's grace…"

Those are His unmerited blessings.

The blood is so important that without the blood there is no redemption. Without the blood, there is no forgiveness. Without the blood there is no remission of sin. Without the blood of Jesus Christ, there is no entrance into Heaven. Without the blood of Jesus Christ in your life, everything we do is null and void. Every song we sing and every word we preach is nothing unless we are covered under the blood of Jesus Christ.

I am convinced the blood actively surrounds you, and God cannot even see your sins because you're covered in the blood of Jesus Christ. When God looks at you, He doesn't even see what you've done wrong, because you're covered under the blood of Jesus Christ.

God had been angry at the condition of man ever since the fall of Adam and Eve. And He's been disappointed. And so, He decided, "I need a sacrifice." Goats, sheep, doves and all those things were used for sacrifices. Sacrifices were made to Him; those things were burned on the altars.

But none of those sacrifices would ever make peace with God. There was only one way.

Colossians 1:20 NASB
"...having made peace through the blood of His cross..."

Through the blood of Jesus Christ, we have made peace with God. We have made peace through the blood of His cross. Without the blood of Jesus Christ covering your life, there is no Salvation. Without the blood of Jesus Christ, there is no access to Heaven. Without the blood of Jesus Christ, you would not be protected and you would not be anointed. Only by the blood of His sacrifice can we have peace with God and have the perfect covering in our life.

Jesus, I have peace in my life because I am at peace with You. I know that my future is in Your hands. I know that Your love has been with me even before I was born. I will live every day of my life confident in my salvation and grateful that You gave Your life for me. Help me live every day as a reflection of You, so that others may see Your love through me. Amen.

Reflections

Conclusion

God gave us one life to live. You are His greatest creation and His desire for you is to build this life to reflect His glory. You are God's beloved and He has given you the greatest opportunity to build a spiritually strong and healthy life. Start today!

Start right now!

Start with the foundation and build upward. Make Jesus the Lord of your life and start building the greatest life you've ever experienced. A life full of peace and comfort. A life full of joy and guidance. God has made a way for us to have an abundant life. It's our choice to allow Him to mold our lives and help us build a strong home.

We all know life is going to happen and life can be difficult. There are trials and problems almost daily.

Life can be discouraging and demanding. However, when you have built your life on the foundation of Jesus Christ, when the winds and storms come ....
YOU WILL PREVAIL!

I won't promise life will be easy all the time but I will promise Jesus will be with you every step of the way. He will never leave us. He will never abandon us. The Bible teaches, "He is a friend who sticks closer than a brother." Even in the worst times, Jesus is still there. When you are **Building a Life** with Jesus, you can navigate through any storm.

Pray this prayer as often as you feel compelled:

"Lord Jesus, I love you. I thank you. I need you. Help me build a life pleasing to you. Help me build a life with You as the foundation. I want you in my life. I confess you as Lord and ask you for guidance. Come into my life and be my Savior. Forgive me for my disobedience. Forgive me for my sins. I thank you for your mercy. I thank you for your grace. Help me to build a life. Amen."

Reflections

_____

_____

_____

_____

_____

_____

_____

_____

_____

_____

_____

_____

published 2018

front cover image:

shutterstock.com

back cover image:

Crystal Day, SouthernDay Photography

Made in the USA
Lexington, KY
19 November 2018